SHIPBUILDING
IN BRITAIN

Fred M. Walker

SHIRE PUBLICATIONS

Published in Great Britain in 2013 by Shire Publications Ltd, Midland House, West Way, Botley, Oxford OX2 0PH, United Kingdom.

43-01 21st Street, Suite 220B, Long Island City, NY 11101, USA.

E-mail: shire@shirebooks.co.uk   www.shirebooks.co.uk

A CIP catalogue record for this book is available from the British Library.

Shire Library no. 565.   ISBN-13: 978 0 74780 729 2

Fred M. Walker has asserted his right under the Copyright, Designs and Patents Act, 1988, to be identified as the author of this book.

Designed by Tony Truscott Designs, Sussex, UK and typeset in Perpetua and Gill Sans.

Printed in China through Worldprint Ltd.

13 14 15 16 17   10 9 8 7 6 5 4 3 2 1

COVER IMAGE
Detail from 'Shipbuilding on the Clyde', a poster produced by Norman Wilkinson for the LNER/LMS, 1923–47. It shows a large ship under construction in the River Clyde shipyards in Scotland.

TITLE PAGE IMAGE
One of the few figureheads fitted in the twentieth century – that of St Sunniva, which sailed to Scotland's Northern Isles and on short cruises. See also page 47.

ACKNOWLEDGEMENTS
Illustrations are acknowledged as follows:

Aberdeen Art Gallery & Museums Collections, pages 1 and 43 (both); Alamy, page 6; GB Marine Art, page 21 (top); Douglas Brown, Gourock, pages 27 and 40 (bottom); Getty Images, pages 22–3 and 54–5; Harland and Wolff, Belfast, pages 30 (top), 46 (both) and 59; HMS Trincomalee Trust, Hartlepool, page 9 (bottom); Manchester Art Gallery/The Bridgeman Art LibraryNational Maritime Museum, Greenwich, page 9 (top); The Royal Institution of Naval Architects, page 44 (bottom); Science and Society Picture Library, cover image; John Swire and Sons, page 48.

Shire Publications is supporting the Woodland Trust, the UK's leading woodland conservation charity, by funding the dedication of trees.

CONTENTS

EARLY SHIPBUILDING IN BRITAIN

SHIPBUILDING is one of the oldest and greatest industries of the United Kingdom, which is not surprising for an island nation with a lengthy coastline and in which few people live more than 50 miles from the sea. In particular, one city, Sunderland, has produced fine ships on the River Wear for more than eight hundred years, while on another river, the Clyde, well over thirty thousand ships were launched in the two hundred years between 1800 and 2000.

The keel of a wooden ship being prepared; the joints should be as few as possible and must be scarfed with great care.

Until the early nineteenth century every ship throughout the world was built of wood, mostly in small shipyards seldom employing more than a couple of dozen people. Such shipbuilding sites required adequate access to

4

the water, and good storage space for stocks of cut timber and uncut lumber. The equipment of the shipyard might comprise no more than a sawpit or trestles for cutting planks with double-ended saws, and a long steam box in which planks could be made pliable by heating up to 100° Celsius, but in addition every worker would own or at least have access to hand tools. An experienced shipwright's toolbox would be a treasure chest containing hammers, axes, an adze, hand saws and a variety of other items accumulated and lovingly cared for during a lifetime of work in ship construction.

It was fairly common for the senior men in these teams – the shipwrights (also known in many places as carpenters) – to be itinerant workers, who used to travel along the coast looking for work, and stay put where it was available. The usual practice was for the proprietor of the business to take a lease on the land required for shipbuilding and then directly employ the workforce of shipwrights, apprentices, helpers and possibly a few others. Other necessary skills would be found nearby, and specialist work would be subcontracted to blacksmiths, rope-makers, riggers and sail-makers. Sizeable ships could be assembled and put to sea in surprisingly few months, a task made easier as ships were then similar in construction, and workmen were expected to know their trade and to work long hours with minimum supervision. In the second half of the twentieth century, when wooden replica ships were built in many parts of

Diagram of a typical scarf joint on a wooden keel.

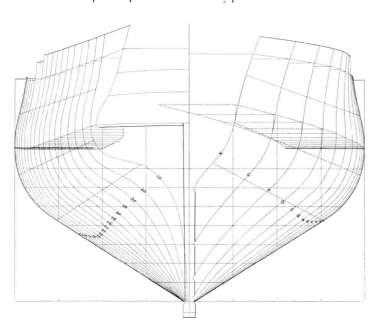

Body plan of a frigate designed by the Thames shipbuilder Marmaduke Stalkartt around 1780.

the world, the tradition of the travelling shipwright was reborn, and teams of highly skilled, dedicated men — and nowadays women — travelled from country to country to build superb traditional wooden hulls.

In the sixteenth century the kings of England and Scotland began to build larger ships for their incipient but underfunded navies, starting a kind of embryonic 'arms race'. This led to the idea of ships dedicated to defence of the realm, and specialist naval bases, which later became the Royal Dockyards, were set up in England for the building and repair of warships: Portsmouth, founded in 1496, remains active; it was followed by Woolwich in 1513 and Chatham in 1547. In these establishments, larger groups of shipyard workers were recruited and employed on a fairly secure basis, and for the first time shipyards using timber developed into big industrial complexes under the management of some of Europe's most talented shipwrights. In the final years of the Tudor dynasty, the Honourable East India Company was founded and granted a monopoly for trading in the East; it set up a large shipyard

The launch at Woolwich Dockyard of the first-rate ship *Royal Albert* in May 1854 by Queen Victoria. This 110-gun ship was one of the largest wooden naval ships of the time and was equipped with both steam and sail propulsion.

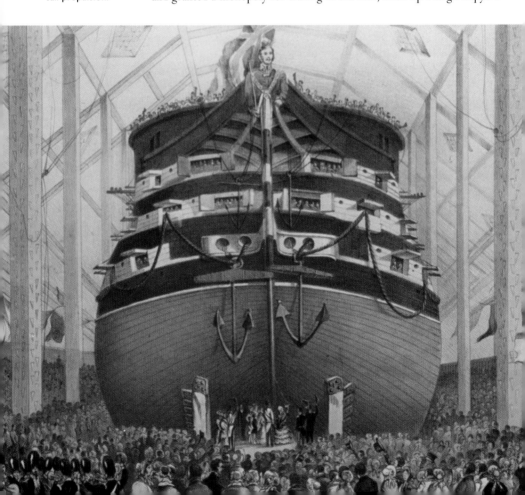

at Blackwall on the River Thames, ensuring that the south of England became the acknowledged centre of shipbuilding expertise for the British Isles. This attracted shipbuilding and allied skills to the area and encouraged many other industries, such as forestry and iron smelting. Following the Act of Union, which united the kingdoms of England and Scotland in 1707, the now-named Royal Navy was regarded highly both at home and overseas and was surpassing the Netherlands as the leading proponent of ship design in

An elegant study by R. H. Penton of the three-masted schooner *Kathleen and May*, dry-docked for annual repairs at Appledore, Devon, in the 1920s.

A timber-hulled ship fully planked and awaiting launch.

Erecting frames for a wooden ship.

Europe — indeed, only the French at that time were serious rivals. In addition to having a steadily growing fleet of warships, Britain was at the forefront of global exploration, led by naval commanders such as James Cook, George Vancouver and Matthew Flinders.

The expansion of the Royal Navy, which had many hundreds of large ships by the time of the Napoleonic Wars, created timber shortages, particularly from England's own forests. Imports from Europe were not always easy in time of war, and supplies from North America were only beginning to be developed. A second problem was that many British rivers had become infested with gribble and Teredo worm, small creatures that attack the underwater timbers of ships' hulls by boring into them, making them unseaworthy in a very short time. An ingenious solution was devised, whereby the Navy arranged an emergency programme of sheathing the underwater parts of all its ships' hulls with copper plating about 1 mm in thickness, giving each hull a clean, 'wetted' surface that protected against borers attacking the submerged timbers, and upon which weed would not grow. This massive undertaking was successful but could not have taken place without an abundant supply

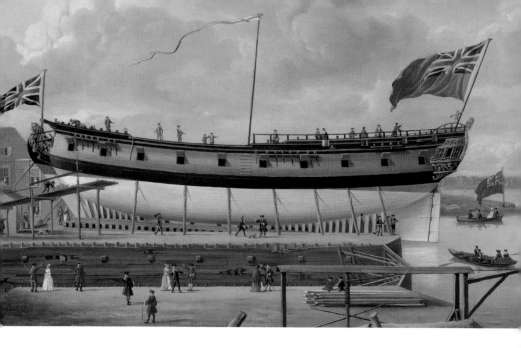

of copper plate from Swansea. The advantage it gave to the Royal Navy was a major factor in the winning of the Napoleonic Wars.

Another problem with wooden ships is that the method of building and the nature of the material effectively limit them to a maximum length of about 80 metres. Few wooden ships have ever been larger, though one exception was a Californian wooden ferry, the *Eureka*, built in 1900, with a length of just over 91 metres. (This ship, which is still afloat, was of unusual construction and has complex internal stiffening of steel king posts and tie rods.) A resolution of this problem eluded naval architects for years and it was only after 1819, when a revolutionary type of ship was constructed using the untried medium of iron, that shipbuilding as we know it now was born.

Preparation for the launch of a sixth-rate ship for the Royal Navy at Deptford Dockyard. Oil painting by John Cleveley the Elder, c. 1750.

Hull coppering on the underside of the 200-year-old frigate HMS *Trincomalee* at Hartlepool; thin copper plates stop marine borers from attacking the hull planking and also prevent the growth of weed, which reduces the operating speed.

STEAM AND IRON

THE TWO most fundamental changes in the history of shipbuilding both occurred in Great Britain in the early nineteenth century as a direct result of the Industrial Revolution. They were the use of steam engines to propel ships, and the introduction of iron as the material for ships' hulls, enabling an almost limitless increase in the size of ships.

Steam power had long been used to assist in land drainage and in the pumping of water from mines. Despite being inefficient and unreliable, the early steam engines were a step forward in an unhurried age, achieving tasks well beyond the capability of human or animal power. The first step in developing high-efficiency machinery began in May 1765 when the Scottish engineer James Watt was strolling on Glasgow Green and pondering a task that was proving difficult – the repair of a working model of a Newcomen engine belonging to Glasgow University. With a flash of inspiration, he realised that the solution was the fitting of a separate steam condenser, and this insight was a key moment in the Industrial Revolution.

By the beginning of the nineteenth century pioneer work had begun on steamships in France, the United States and Scotland. The first British steamships were two canal tugs, *Charlotte Dundas 1* and *2*, which operated less than successfully on the Forth & Clyde Canal in the early 1800s, but real history was made in 1812 when the *Comet* became the first steamship in regular operation in Europe, carrying passengers between Glasgow and Helensburgh. The *Comet* was driven by twin paddles on each side, powered by a simple steam engine using gear invented by Watt (shown overleaf) to convert the oscillating strokes of the engine into rotary motion. The engine was so inefficient that it required 100 tons of coal to obtain the theoretical work of 1 ton of coal, and as the *Comet* was only 13 metres long it was able to carry enough fuel for only a short voyage. Fifty years would pass before the 'thermal efficiency' of marine power plants became high enough, and hulls large enough, for ships to steam from London to the Far East economically. However, the *Comet* in 1812 had cast the die, and British shipyards realised that a new market lay with steamships.

Opposite: Detail from *A Ship for Canada in a United Kingdom Shipyard*, a poster painted by Charles Pears, dating from the 1920s or 1930s. The vessel is presumably being prepared for launching as most of the construction work is complete.

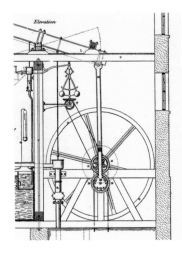

A double-acting engine showing Watt's ball governor and sun-and-planet gearing.

Early-nineteenth-century naval architects were well aware of the current timber shortages, although, knowing of no construction material other than timber, they may not have appreciated the immutable and little understood limitation of about 80 metres for hull length. Most were concerned that wooden ships were subject to rot and decay, especially if built hurriedly of 'green' or under-seasoned wood and then subjected to hard wear and inadequate maintenance. An example of this was the Russian sailing fleet on the Baltic at the beginning of the nineteenth century: its ships lasted little more than six years on average, owing to the poor quality of western Russian timber, the annual six-month lay-up when the brackish water of the Gulf of Finland was frozen over, and poor maintenance. Conversely, the British ships in the Royal Navy lasted longer as they were out at sea for much of the year, were built of English or Scots oak, and generally were well maintained. Wooden ships are better preserved when operating in the sea rather than in fresh water.

By the 1780s ironfounding had become an established part of the British industrial scene and one man with an infectious enthusiasm for iron, John 'Iron Mad' Wilkinson, promoted its use in unexpected ways: he manufactured iron window frames and pillars for house building; he gifted iron pulpits to local churches; and sometimes, in doubtful taste, he would present unsuspecting young ladies with iron coffins. He was probably the first man to have used iron in the construction of a small ship – a craft no larger than a modern English canal narrowboat – when his canalside foundry had difficulties maintaining adequate supplies of coal and ore at a time when the local boatbuilders were slow in delivery. He took matters into his own hands and built a simple box-shaped structure capable of transporting his cargoes; it had an elementary timber frame of oak and elm, with an outer skin of iron plates, similar to the swim-headed barges later used on the Thames. Details are unclear, but it is reputed to have been built about 1787, named *Trial*

William Symington's pioneering steamship *Charlotte Dundas II.*

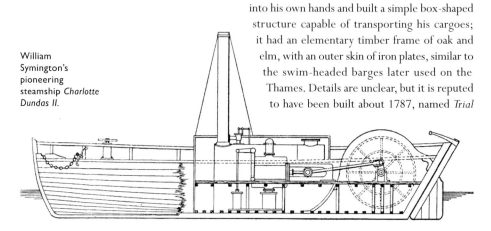

and measured about 20 metres long, with a breadth of no more than 2 metres for canal operation. Nothing is known of its history.

The real introduction of iron to shipbuilding came in 1819, when the Forth & Clyde Canal Company built a fast horse-drawn 'passage barge', which operated daily carrying passengers between Edinburgh and Glasgow. This deep-water canal crossed Scotland from sea to sea and, being a successful commercial venture, it suffered from traffic congestion and the associated problems of damage to the hundreds of craft operating on it. Around 1815 a group of engineers and scientists convened to study the problem (including James Watt, Professor Joseph Black of Glasgow – the discoverer of latent heat, and John Schank, a British admiral noted for lateral thinking) and they proposed the revolutionary idea of building the new hull of iron. Thomas Wilson, a shipwright with no previous experience of ironwork, was commissioned to construct this fast barge, being instructed to build her in traditional, 'ship-shaped' form. The planning took three years, while the actual construction took less than one year, and in 1819, to the amazement of the bystanders, the appropriately named *Vulcan* was launched sideways into the Monklands Canal near Glasgow. It was an overnight success and this 20-metre hull was to remain in gainful employment for over fifty years. Its suitability for the job and its historic importance can be measured in three ways:

• It established a method of construction that is used by all shipyards throughout the world to this day.
• It enabled ships to break through the 'length barrier' imposed by timber construction. (It was announced in 2011 that a class of twelve fast container ships, ordered by a Danish company from a South Korean shipyard, will have the unprecedented length of 400 metres, more than twenty times longer than the pioneering *Vulcan*.)

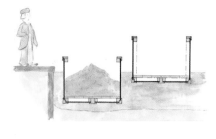

Above: Probable cross-section of John Wilkinson's barge *Trial* of 1787.

Left: Thomas Wilson (1781–1873), the builder of the world's first properly built iron ship, the *Vulcan* of 1819.

The pioneer fast iron passage barge *Vulcan* of 1819. This ship was the progenitor of all subsequent iron and steel ships, but was different in that the strakes were vertical instead of horizontal.

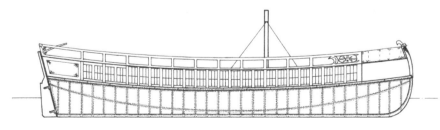

The pioneer iron screw collier *John Bowes*, built by Palmer's Shipbuilding and Iron Company of Jarrow in 1852. This ship modernised freight transport and had a successful career spanning eighty-one years. This historic photograph shows *John Bowes* passing the gantry cranes of the shipyard in which she was constructed.

• The operating experience with this new ship confirmed that iron hulls are long-lasting, some now having survived more than a hundred years.

Iron ship construction and marine steam propulsion were revolutionary, and within thirty years the shipbuilding industries had changed beyond recognition, with possibly a score of ironworking shipyards set up on new sites or converted from former timber shipbuilding yards. In 1838 the Bristol-built iron steamship *Great Britain*, the brainchild of Isambard Kingdom Brunel and driven by an evolutionary screw propeller, set new standards in the design and appearance of sea-going ships. Iron enabled

The heavy riveted stern plates of the SS *Great Britain* (1837), now restored at her birthplace in Bristol.

Below: The London river collier or flatiron was a remarkable type of ship designed to carry coal from Scotland and the north-east of England to the capital. Its design enabled it to remain on a level keel and pass under the London bridges at high tide when laden and at low tide when in ballast.

shipbuilders to demonstrate imaginative engineering skills, such as the introduction of water ballast tanks that were integral parts of the hull and obviated the need for loose ballast in ships' holds. Such tanks enabled the colliers sailing from north-eastern ports with coal to London to take on ballast quickly when the cargo had been discharged and to return northwards sooner for a further cargo of sea coal.

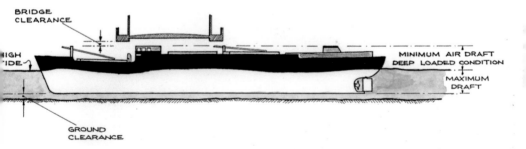

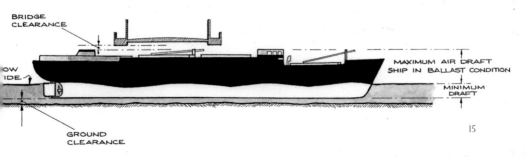

SAILING SHIPS FIGHT BACK

DESPITE ADVANCES IN THE STEAM ENGINE, sailing ships continued to be built; their cheapness of operation appealed to shipowners, and throughout the nineteenth century shipyards produced three- and four-masted barques of iron (and later steel). Some were large enough to lift a cargo of over 6,000 tonnes and to operate in all parts of the world, manned by overworked and scandalously underpaid crews of about twenty men. Their efficiency came from being able to carry a cargo deadweight equivalent to 74 or 75 per cent of their full displacement. One of the last of these great sailers was the *Archibald Russell*, launched by Scott's of Greenock in 1905.

The composite-built tea clipper *Coral Nymph*, built by William Pile of Sunderland in 1864. A ship portrait of the Chinese school.

The mid-nineteenth century was the heyday of the fast sailing ships known as tea clippers. This fleet of just over one hundred vessels excited public imagination for a short, romantic period of thirty years, which ended with the opening of the Suez Canal in 1869. Each year the clippers loaded up with the new tea crop in Chinese ports and then raced to London, every captain hoping to be the first home, to win a prestigious prize and to sell his precious cargo at a premium. The development of a straight stem and hollow lines forward by the shipbuilder Alexander Hall introduced the world to the 'Aberdeen bow', and two of the shipyards in that city (Alexander Hall's and Walter Hood's) began to build ultra-fast sailing ships. Their main competitors were three shipyards on the Clyde – Charles Connell, A. & J. Inglis and Robert Steele. Only a few clippers were built in England – mainly at Liverpool and Sunderland, with a couple from London. The two outstanding ships were the *Thermopylae*, built by Walter Hood of Aberdeen, and the *Cutty Sark*, built by Scott & Linton of Dumbarton and now docked permanently at Greenwich in her home port of London.

The clippers were built of wood as it was found that the insides of the holds did not sweat on the return voyage to Britain, while ships built of iron generated large quantities of condensation on the inside of the shell plating, with an adverse effect on the cargo of tea. To ensure the ships were as long, strong and capacious as possible, many clipper ships had their keels and frames (their skeletal structure) built of iron, and then had their shells constructed of hardwood – teak and continental oak being favourites. Such vessels were known as 'composite ships', and only three (all British-built) now survive: the *Cutty Sark* in Greenwich; the auxiliary sloop HMS *Gannet*, which was built in Sheerness Dockyard and is now exhibited at the Historic Dockyard in Chatham; and the sailing passenger ship *City of Adelaide*, which was built in the nineteenth century by William Pile of Sunderland and is now on the Clyde awaiting transportation to South Australia for restoration.

Builder's half-block model of the tea clipper *Coulnakyle*, built by Alexander Hall of Aberdeen in 1862. The unique Aberdeen bow is apparent.

The glass-sided tank developed by Alexander Hall, containing water covered by red turpentine. Hall compared models by towing them through the tank, and he adjudged those that had the least turbulent flow to be the best.

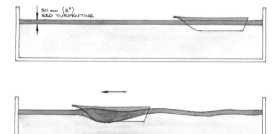

THE HEYDAY OF BRITISH SHIPBUILDING

BY 1880 most ships being constructed in Britain, and indeed in Europe, were of iron. In a mere sixty years this material had been mastered: the workforce was accustomed to it, and machine tools of ever increasing power were being used in the yards. Iron is a good shipbuilding material as it is slow to corrode by oxidation (rusting) and iron hulls are long lasting, but during the nineteenth century experiments revealed that if small quantities of other metals were added to molten iron then the alloys formed would have much greater strength. These alloys, known as steels, were used on small and experimental ships from around the 1850s – generally without success, owing to the high cost of these steels and their poor resistance to rusting and abrasion. It was only in the 1870s that means were found of manufacturing steel in bulk and at reasonable cost, so that it could be used in shipbuilding. In 1879 the first large steel ship, the 8,000-ton cattle and cargo carrier SS *Buenos Ayrean*, was produced by Denny of Dumbarton. This signalled the start of the changeover in British shipyards to the use of steel. Initially the cost of building was higher but, as steel production increased throughout the English and Scottish mills, costs fell and by 1890 almost all ships were of steel. Britain was then ten years ahead of every other country, producing ships of greater strength, and with a 10 per cent reduction in material weight that enabled greater cargoes or larger fuel bunkers to be carried. The changeover cost was minimal as machine tools and working practices were unchanged.

Shipbuilding output, like that of most heavy industries, is cyclical. On looking at the tonnage output of the years, one sees sharp dips in years of economic depression, counterbalanced by some amazingly high peaks of production. In 1913, the year before the outbreak of the First World War, British shipbuilders experienced unparalleled success, the annual returns showing 1,460 ships (of over 2 million gross tons) launched throughout Great Britain and Ireland – ships of every type, mostly of steel with screw propulsion, but with still a few built with timber and propelled by sails or paddle wheels. Steam reciprocating machinery, having just reached a peak of efficiency, powered the vast bulk of ships under construction, but two new features of marine engineering were emerging: steam turbines and marine diesels. Effectively invented by Sir Charles Parsons and developed at Wallsend-on-Tyne, steam turbines were being fitted to passenger ships of all sizes from the swift river steamers on the Firth of Clyde through to the giant Atlantic record breakers. The large marine diesel was then in its infancy, being developed by the Danish shipbuilders and engineers Burmeister & Wain of Copenhagen. The first three ocean-going diesel-powered ships were the *Selandia*, the *Jutlandia* and the *Fionia*, two of them built in Copenhagen and one by the Barclay, Curle shipyard in Glasgow. It is impossible to overrate the importance of these early contracts, for nowadays around 99 per cent of all ships worldwide have diesel machinery.

During this amazing year around seventy ships were built for the Royal Navy or other government departments, including two battleships, four cruisers and a clutch of submarines. About half were built in commercial shipyards, and the remainder in the Royal Dockyards of Portsmouth, Devonport, Chatham and Pembroke. The merchant shipbuilders felt always that they were at a disadvantage to the Royal Dockyards, which were funded centrally by the government and to some extent cushioned financially. However, at that time, when government policy decreed that the Royal Navy had to be greater in size than the world's second and third largest fleets put together, there was a strong argument in favour of their operation. In addition, the Royal Dockyards provided continuous maintenance and repair for a fleet that operated worldwide and was in a state of high readiness. Portsmouth in particular has one remarkable claim to fame, in that the battleship HMS *Dreadnought*, the first of a revolutionary class of warship, was built there in 1906 in the astonishing time of 366 days.

Submarine construction had been underway in Britain since 1901, and surprisingly Britain was then more committed to this type of craft than were the Germans, as an examination of the statistics shows that at the outbreak of the First World War Germany had only fifteen boats, whilst the United Kingdom had seventy-four. (In naval circles submarines are referred to not as 'ships' but as 'boats'.) Of these, nearly three-quarters had been built at Barrow-in-Furness by Vickers, Son & Maxim, a shipyard later renamed Vickers, and in more recent years known as BAE Systems. A few had come from Chatham Dockyard, and a few from Scott's of Greenock,

The pioneer turbine passenger steamer *King Edward*, built for passenger services on the Clyde coast by Denny of Dumbarton in 1901. It had the first steam turbines (Parsons design) ever fitted to a commercial ship, and had five propellers fitted initially, as shown in this model in Glasgow Museums.

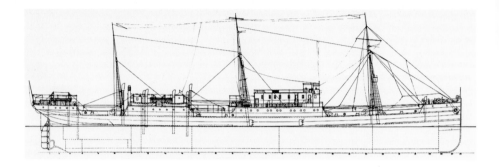

Built by Barclay, Curle of Glasgow in 1912 for the East Asiatic Company of Copenhagen, the twin-screw *Jutlandia* was the first motor ship built in Britain, and the second in the world. The early motor ships for Scandinavia avoided the use of traditional funnels.

which continued building them until the 1970s. This excellent background in submarine construction would stand Britain well in the coming years of conflict, when some amazing craft would come from the shipyards, including the ill-fated steam-driven boat K13, built by Fairfield of Govan, Glasgow, which sank in Gare Loch during trials in January 1917. A massive effort mounted by the Navy and the Clyde shipyards saved forty-six of the seventy-seven men aboard, including William Wallace, who as Sir William became one of Britain's most distinguished engineers and invented the steam catapult, and Percy Hillhouse, one of the shipyard naval architects and later professor of naval architecture at Glasgow University.

Of the 1,460 ships built in 1913, an amazing 367 (or 25 per cent) came from the Clyde – more than one for every day of the year. The Clyde's greatest launch was the Cunard liner *Aquitania*, known as the 'Ship Beautiful', then the largest ship in the world and almost the last built in Britain with four elegant funnels. It operated successfully for the following thirty-six years, working as

The engine shop of Hall, Russell of Aberdeen in the 1960s with two Fredriksstad steam compound engines under construction. After this, machinery construction ceased and the main diesel engines were bought in from large engine suppliers.

a troopship in both world wars. However, every shipbuilding region made a valuable contribution, notably the north-east of England, where yards on the three great rivers Tyne, Tees and Wear, and also at Hartlepool, produced hundreds of steam freighters, many known as 'three-island ships', which equipped the fleets of many nations, but especially the British Merchant Marine – then the largest in the world. It has been said that many tramp ships, when completed on the Tyne or Wear, would pick up their first cargo of steaming coal in South Wales for delivery to one of Britain's strategically placed coaling stations. Work would then follow on the cross trades, taking cargo wherever offered in the world, finally coming home to the United Kingdom some years later, having picked up a seasonal cargo of grain for Britain or western Europe from the River Plate. A deck apprentice officer might serve his full time of around four years on one single voyage.

The Cunard liner *Aquitania* – known as 'The Ship Beautiful' on sea-trials in the Firth of Clyde, May 1914. This magnificent ship, then the largest in the world, was built by John Brown of Clydebank and was to serve continuously until withdrawn from service in 1950.

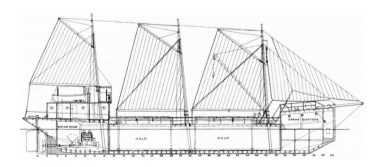

Proposed design for a concrete coastal ship, 1920. Concrete was introduced around the time of the First World War but made little headway as a shipbuilding material.

The *Aquitania* seen afloat at the outfitting quay of John Brown's shipyard some time after her launch on 21 April 1913. One of the problems of a shipyard is finding temporary storage space near a ship for the myriad items that require to be placed aboard in an ordered sequence. The Ship Manager must also ensure that moorings are secure, fire precautions are up to the mark and all walkways and working areas made safe.

THE WORLD WARS

THE FOUR YEARS of the First World War (1914–18) marked the beginning of the end of Britain's pre-eminence in shipbuilding. Initially many shipyard workers volunteered for the Army and were drafted to the Western Front, but this potential labour shortage was stopped and soon the shipyards were working at full capacity, and the workforce – from draughtsman to director, from shipwright to superintendent – applied themselves with the confidence of men acknowledged as the best in the world at their job. The strain of working against the clock and of continuous repairs to vessels that had survived attack by enemy ships and submarines began to take a toll, however, and the entry of the United States into the war in 1917 came as a relief, especially as the Americans commenced an admirable programme of shipbuilding for the Allied cause.

With the return of peace in 1919, the shipyards began to replace lost ships and to restart their export business. For a while it seemed that life had returned to normal, but after just a few years orders began to dry up and British shipbuilders faced the first real long-term downturn for over thirty years. The problem was compounded by the loss in the war of many potential leaders of the industry, by former regular clients placing their orders elsewhere, and by the poor image that shipbuilding acquired during the years of depression, which deterred the recruitment of senior staff. By 1933 only 5 per cent of Britain's shipbuilding capacity was being utilised and the industry was plagued with wasteful competition as shipbuilders tried to attract orders by offering loss-making prices. Long-established yards began to close – the most significant being the Palmers Shipbuilding & Iron Company Ltd of Jarrow, a massive combine that imported iron ore to the Tyne and ultimately delivered large warships. The name of its home town has become irrevocably associated with the Jarrow March, when unemployed shipyard workers and others drew public attention to the desperate plight of the out-of-work.

The shipbuilding industry made a brave but controversial attempt to overcome the problem of surplus capacity and ruinous competition.

Opposite:
Wartime damage to the tanker *Imperial Transport*. During the Second World War, repairs such as this were everyday occurrences.

The Norwegian royal yacht *Norge*. Built by Camper & Nicholson's at Southampton in 1937 as the *Philante*, she was purchased after the Second World War and converted to her current role.

Existing shipyards paid a small levy to a company known as National Shipbuilders Security Ltd, which in turn bought out inefficient shipbuilding berths and 'sterilised' them, thereby reducing building potential by about one-third in the 1930s. A few other yards were mothballed or retained in 'suspended animation' for strategic reasons, including the possibility of future war. In the late 1930s the shipyards came back to life as the economy improved; the government subsidised the building of the two Cunard White Star 'Queen' liners for the North Atlantic ferry service, and also placed orders for an increasing amount of naval work, as the threat of war with Nazi Germany loomed.

The shipbuilding industry was ready for the Second World War (1939–45), a strategy having been prepared over some years by the Shipbuilding Conference representing shipyard proprietors. The government appointed directors of building for the merchant and naval fleets, with authority to place orders with whichever shipyards were best suited and equipped to carry out such work. Large numbers of escort craft were ordered, all of standard designs, such as the two hundred or so 'Flower' Class corvettes, which were based on the successful whale-catcher design of Smith's Dock at Middlesbrough. Another innovation was the unconventional means of building numerous small harbour tugs known as TIDs for the Army and the Royal Navy; each had five prefabricated units made at different inland factory sites and then assembled, tested and commissioned for service at a waterside location.

During the Second World War the Royal Navy lost over one thousand ships to enemy action, and the British and Allied merchant navies over five thousand. This could not have been made good without the very active help of the United States and without the drive and determination of the shipbuilding industry. Every day large convoys of ships returned to Liverpool on the Mersey and to Glasgow and Greenock on the Clyde (as well as many other ports), damaged by torpedo, mine or aircraft attack, and these had to be accorded scarce dry-dock facilities and speedily repaired for return to sea. Ship repairing became an especially stressful round-the-clock activity.

Following the entry of the United States into the war in 1941, it was agreed that shipbuilding production in North America would major on cargo ships, whilst the United Kingdom would concentrate to a greater extent on military craft. The Americans were as good as their word and set up new yards geared to prefabricate and mass-produce the standard-design freighters needed to replace the ships lost in the Nazi U-boat campaign. In all they

Based on the whale-catcher design developed by Smith's Dock of Middlesbrough, the standardised Second World War corvettes were built in large numbers by British and Canadian shipyards. HMS *Arabis*, built by George Brown of Greenock in 1943, was one of hundreds of these small vessels that acted as convoy escorts throughout the war.

A shipyard working at full tilt in 1949. The Fairfield Basin at Govan in Glasgow welcomes a newly launched ship alongside two liners being restored after punishing wartime duty.

built several thousand freighters from a group of half a dozen designs, notably the 'Liberty ship', or EC2-S-C1 type, developed from an original design prepared by the Sunderland shipyard of Joseph Thompson & Sons. All these American ships were welded 100 per cent throughout and this form of construction became (and remains) the norm in all shipyards, the new trade of welder having entered the ranks of shipbuilders during the 1920s and 1930s. For Britain there was no turning back, and on the return of peace all British shipyards invested in welding, which by the 1960s was commonplace in the industry.

POST-WAR HISTORY

L IKE OTHER INDUSTRIES at the end of the Second World War, shipbuilding faced unprecedented demands as shipowners rushed to rebuild their fleets following massive losses to the enemy. There was no hardship in that perhaps, but, with raw-material shortages and shipyards struggling with machinery that had worked non-stop in the war years, this period was far from easy, and there was no let-up. Too much effort was put into replacing the world fleet, while insufficient thought was given to the long-term future of the industry. During the war some overseas customers had found alternative sources of supply, while other countries had developed their own indigenous industry, a situation exacerbated by the re-entry to the market of the Germans and Japanese with fully reconstructed, state-of-the-art shipyards. The nemesis of British shipbuilding was in sight by the 1960s, when, for the first time in nearly a century, the United Kingdom was overtaken in the international shipbuilding stakes by Japan, and after that by Germany, the People's Republic of China, India and the ultra-efficient shipyards of South Korea.

Britain did build a wide range of excellent ships until the 1990s, and two special ventures are worthy of mention. The first was the long and successful run of 'standard' ships, designed as a replacement for the American Liberty ships, which by then were outdated. The design was known initially as the SD14, of which nearly two hundred were built in two or three yards, with Austin & Pickersgill of Sunderland taking the lead. The second exciting development was the ship factory developed by Doxford of Sunderland, but given no encouragement by a Conservative government wishing to replace it with a car plant that was not otherwise allowed by European Union rules.

The first major inquiry into shipbuilding, the Geddes Report, took place during 1965 and 1966 and proposed that shipyards operate in groupings such as the River Tyne, Sunderland and the Wear, the east coast of Scotland, the upper Clyde and the lower Clyde. There were many fallings-out and with the nationalisation of the industry in 1977 several less efficient plants were closed, resulting in a fairly small industry in Britain. The subsequent

Highly skewed controllable pitch (or feathering) propellers on a new roll-on/roll-off ship. (Harland & Wolff)

An amazing ship repair – the side trawler *Bannockburn* was rammed in the North Sea while acting as an oil-rig security vessel. The damage was contained within one of the deep tanks, and the ship was able to make port before being slipped for repair.

denationalisation or break-up of a tiny industry was unwanted and was an unmitigated disaster, with highly efficient shipyards in Aberdeen, Sunderland and elsewhere closed for ever. Now, shipbuilding is concentrated in just a few sites – at Barrow-in-Furness, at Glasgow and Port Glasgow, at Portchester in Hampshire, and at Appledore in Devon. Most of the work is for military vessels – destroyers, submarines and aircraft carriers.

In addition there are several small shipyards engaged in both repairs and construction, such as the Buckie shipyard in Aberdeenshire and Nielsen's shipyard in Gloucester, which specialises in wooden and restored craft. Long gone are the days when in the annual trade returns one could count the names of a hundred shipyards spread across the length and breadth of Britain. However, despite this reduction in the number of new ships, their quality is as good as ever, with many ships being built in an unusual manner; one such method is the importing of empty steel hulls from eastern European shipyards to be fitted out and then equipped with propulsion machinery in the United Kingdom.

DESIGN AND MODEL TESTING

Designing a new ship is an exciting project dependent upon good teamwork. Techniques have changed over the past two hundred years, but the principles have remained the same right into the age of computers. With substantial increases in ship size and the need for precision, it became essential for shipyards to develop design systems and to be able to produce good working plans. With the change to iron construction, shipyards set up drawing offices staffed by experienced draughtsmen, and design offices manned by professional engineers – now known as naval architects. In the early days the plans for a ship could be produced easily in a matter of weeks, but, as scientific knowledge expanded and ships became more complicated, this process became lengthier.

The greatest problem facing naval architects was how to estimate the size, power and fuel consumption of the machinery needed to propel a ship at the contracted speed. Despite the efforts of eminent scientists, these objectives remained elusive until in the 1870s the world was presented with the work of William Froude. Froude (pronounced 'Frood') had studied at Oriel College, Oxford, and then practised engineering under some distinguished men, including I. K. Brunel. He retired early, ostensibly to care for his ailing father, but, as the family was more than comfortably off, it was apparent that he wished to spend time on private research. He was intrigued by the question of how to forecast a ship's power, and made a variety of scale model ships for systematic testing in the static water of garden pools and duck ponds. His incisive brain led him to believe that there was a fairly simple mathematical relationship between the power required to 'steam' a full-size ship and the power required for a small scale model, or 'geosim'. His powers of persuasion were equal to his intellect, and the Lords of the Admiralty encouraged him and allowed him the use of two Royal Navy sloops, the *Greyhound* and the *Alert*, for testing at sea. Froude used the *Alert* as a tug and carefully recorded the power expended in towing *Greyhound* through the water, in a series of experiments that continued for many months. Then, with some financial backing from the Admiralty, he built a ship-model test

William Froude
(1810–79),
remembered
as the greatest
hydrodynamicist
of all time.

tank (something similar to a small roofed-over swimming pool) at Torquay, where he continued the same tests and experiments on small-scale geosims of *Greyhound*.

Froude had realised that ships, while moving through water, have to overcome first the frictional resistance between the hull and the water, and then the substantial resistance caused by the energy absorbed in creating the wave patterns around the ship. While it may sound as if the problem had become greater, Froude saw it otherwise and with a skilful mathematical approach developed what is now known as Froude's Law of Comparisons, which was published in 1874. This work is regarded as one of the greatest scientific achievements of the nineteenth century and helped establish Britain as shipbuilder to the world.

In 1844 a small shipyard was established in Dumbarton, an historic town 15 miles west of Glasgow; the yard of William Denny & Brothers continued production until 1962, by which time it had built over 1,500 ships, many of which were amongst the best in the world. The third William Denny was enthusiastic about Froude's work and persuaded his partners to build a ship-model test tank, which, he believed, would give them a head start on all their competitors. It came into commission in 1883. (The test tank, the world's oldest surviving example and the prototype of hundreds in other countries, remains in operating condition and is managed by the Scottish Maritime Museum.) In the early 1880s the Belgian government required especially fast paddle steamers for the Dover to Ostend service and issued invitations to tender for this work. Few shipyards were interested, owing to the stringency of the contract, but, having invested much research effort, including use of their test tank, Denny's were awarded the contract for PS *Princesse Henriette* – an outstanding fast cross-Channel ship that established the Dumbarton shipyard as an acknowledged world leader, a position it would hold for seventy years.

To serve an apprenticeship with Denny's, especially in the drawing office, was regarded on the Clyde as an honour – even more so if one was

Drawing from the 1870s showing the method used by Froude to calculate the power required to move HMS *Greyhound* through the sea.

The ship-model test tank at Glasgow University. To ensure that experimental results are as sensitive as possible, the carriage rails on either side of the tank are shaped to reflect the earth's curvature.

An early export job: the Japanese armoured screw corvette *Jo Sho Maru*, launched by Alexander Hall of Aberdeen in 1864 as a speculative building for the Japanese Imperial Navy; this ship lasted forty years and was broken up in 1904.

a university undergraduate. Apprentice draughtsmen worked at a long drawing board, on which they learned to produce scale ship plans, under the watchful eyes of qualified 'journeymen'. Shipyards retained and indexed plans from previous ships, and apprentices were encouraged to study these and learn from them. It was a matter of honour that any

The ship drawing office of Denny of Dumbarton around 1956.

advanced scientific projects upon which Denny's was engaged were never discussed outside the shipyard.

The drawing boards were about 3 metres long and the edge nearest the draughtsman was straight and true, enabling a tee-square to set up parallel lines across the board as required. The length is surprising until one realises that in former days the plans (possibly scaled at ¼ inch to the foot, or 1/48) would be for the complete deck of a ship, so that if the deck were 400 feet long the plan would be close to 3 metres in length. The plans were drawn in pencil or in black ink on very fine, smooth and starched linen cloth.

As the trainee progressed through apprenticeship and passed more examinations at night school, day release or university, there was an incentive to spend time in the naval architect's office, known in some older shipyards as the Scientific Department. Here work was hard, with

Lines plan of a single-screw steam tug.

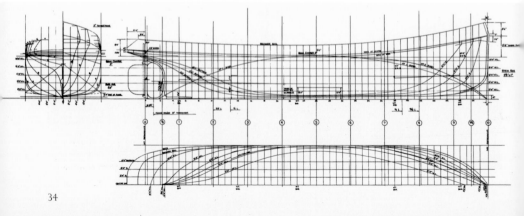

A draughtsman
preparing a
lines plan.

considerable time having to be spent on unending calculations, or 'number
crunching'. In the days before electric or electronic calculators, such work
had to be carried out in set forms, but with the help of log tables, slide rules
and the most accurate tool of them all – the hand-held barrel slide rule.

Ship design is scientific rather than artistic, but the naval architect is still
responsible for ensuring that a newly built ship is imbued with grace

Before the
introduction of
computers, the
most advanced
design aid in the
naval architect's
office was
the integrator.

The Cunard liner *Queen Elizabeth 2* at anchor off Queensferry on the Firth of Forth.

and elegance. In the 1960s, when the *Queen Elizabeth 2* was being designed at John Brown's of Clydebank, meetings were attended by the future owners Cunard, by James Gardner (an industrial designer) and by the shipyard naval architects; the result was a ship of great elegance. Interior designers are consulted regularly to ensure that passenger and crew accommodation is restful and will not become dated. The interior accommodation must be designed to allow for the camber or transverse rounding of decks, as well as the sheer or concavity from bow to stern.

The design of funnel can be controversial; it should be of simple and clean, but distinctive design, and it must throw exhaust gases well clear of the upper decks. In earlier years the funnel was supplied by the engineers – a tradition from the days when a tall smokestack, designed to give good draught for the furnaces, was part of the machinery. By tradition the funnel colours of the Cunard Line (red with black hoops and a black top) were the trademark of Robert Napier, the Clydeside engineer who supplied the engines for Samuel Cunard's first four transatlantic ships, built in four different Clyde shipyards in 1840.

Diagram explaining sheer, draft and freeboard.

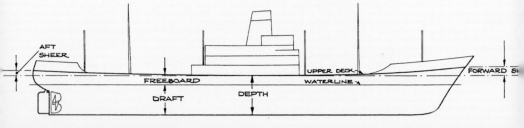

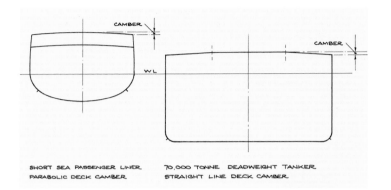

Diagram explaining camber on modern ships.

SHORT SEA PASSENGER LINER
PARABOLIC DECK CAMBER

70,000 TONNE DEADWEIGHT TANKER
STRAIGHT LINE DECK CAMBER

The funnels (or smokestacks) of the Clyde passenger steamer *Queen Alexandra*, built in 1912. This demonstrates clearly that funnels in earlier days were for improved furnace draught and were part of the engineering department's responsibility.

THE CONSTRUCTION
PROCESS

IN THE 1830s and 1840s many old wooden shipyards were converting to work with iron, and their workforce developed the new skills of using heat and force to bend strong metal to shape, whilst ensuring each manufactured part was a precise match for its neighbour. Shipbuilding may have become a noisy and tough business, but it had graduated into a precision industry. In 1833 an up-and-coming iron shipbuilder, John Laird of Birkenhead, received an order for a paddle steamer from the Inland Steam Navigation Company of Ireland. This was a feather in Laird's cap as his business had been in existence for less than twenty years and he had been building iron ships for less than four. Despite being only 40 metres in length, the new ship, *Lady Landsdowne*, was too large to sail through the canals and rivers of the Irish midlands, and other means of delivery had to be found. Instead of riveting the ship during construction, it was held together by temporary bolts, and all parts were clearly marked and numbered before being dismantled and crated for shipping across the Irish Sea, for re-erection and final riveting at her new home port. It is possible that this was the first ever example of 'knock-down' shipbuilding, a system used by British shipyards until just after the Second World War and which accounted for a small but significant part of the country's exports. (Knock-down shipbuilding has also been called 'Meccano shipbuilding', but accountants use the more prosaic term 'shipment job'.) Laird's continued to build many well-known craft, notably the *John Randolph*, the first iron steamship to operate in the United States, and the shallow-draft river steamer *Ma Roberts*, built for the missionary Dr David Livingstone's exploration and anti-slavery work in Africa.

Building the earliest iron ships with riveted construction must have been experimental, but within a few years systems of shipbuilding evolved that were to become standard throughout Britain. First, when all planning was complete, the iron plates and sections would be ordered from the rolling mills, which included the great steelworks of Middlesbrough, Motherwell, Scunthorpe, Port Talbot and elsewhere. The plates were rolled to exact thickness and then cut to

Opposite:
The view across the double bottom of the great liner *Queen Elizabeth* while under construction at Clydebank. The first part of the keel of this ship was laid in December 1936 and just twenty-one months later the hull was sufficiently complete for launching to take place on 27 September 1938.

A sketch of the African river paddle steamer *Helen Saker* built in Glasgow in 1875 for the London Missionary Society.

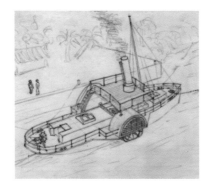

size within agreed tolerances before being despatched by rail to the shipyards. On arrival, the iron plates and sections were stored and allowed to rust, ensuring mill scale and similar detritus would be 'weathered' off the plate, before it was wire-brushed and painted with red lead. Owing to the size and weight of plates, most stockyards had rail tracks and mobile cranes.

Many people are surprised that the midship section (or middle cut) of conventional ships is close to square in shape, but understand that the more shaped parts are towards the bow and the stern. The task of issuing instructions as to the exact shape, curvature and bevel of every part of the ship was the responsibility of those working in the mould loft, where the lines of the ship were laid out on the floor at full size, and templates and patterns were manufactured and working instructions prepared. The complexity of these tasks is underlined when one appreciates that many

A 'knock-down' vessel under construction at the Greenock shipyard of George Brown in 1925.

shell plates have double curvature and most shell frames are not only shaped but can have altering bevels throughout their length. Loft work has changed over the years, most dramatically in the 1950s, when, after much planning and staff training, it was changed to one-tenth scale, and again in the 1970s, when the full task was carried out using computer programs.

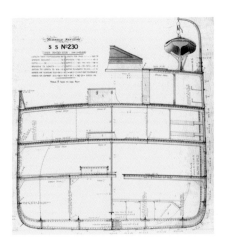

In the preparation shops each plate was cut to size using guillotines that could slice through iron or steel up to 50 mm thick; it was then bent using rollers or mangles, and had rivet holes drilled in position or sometimes punched out by mechanical processes. Each plate had a unique identification number and was clearly marked whether port or starboard. The individual parts were assembled at the building berth, and here the ship was pulled together piece by piece and connected by temporary bolts. On completion of significant parts, the final fasteners were fixed – the red-hot rivets were hammered into position and, when cooled, formed an almost unbreakable bond between the plates. As the

Midship section plan of the SS *Wingsang*, built for the Indo China Steam Navigation Company at Aberdeen in 1883.

The steel stockyard of a Clyde shipyard in the early twentieth century.

41

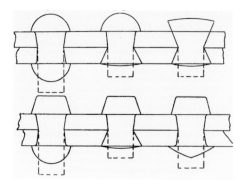

Details of rivets from *Walton's Steel Ships*.

ship took shape, walkways, scaffolding (known in the shipyards as staging) and safety rails were fitted, and a close eye was kept on items that had to be placed aboard before access became impossible. Painting now proceeded, and the positions of pipes and cables were marked out before the task of outfitting or ship furnishing commenced.

In the nineteenth century most large shipyards tried to limit the work contracted out and they had many departments, including painters, joiners, upholsterers and, in the larger shipyards, model makers. The joiners were especially important as their work, akin to the craft of the cabinet maker, would catch the eye of potential purchasers. In the 1880s a new trade, and a new department, was created following the successful installation of electrical lighting on the Clyde-built Inman liner *City of Berlin*. While this spelt the end for antiquated lighting on ships and the passing of the old trade of lamp trimmer, it also introduced better lighting in the shipyard and on the building berths. The size of electrical departments expanded rapidly and by the 1920s ships that were electrical from masthead to keel were being built.

Riveting on the side of the Cunard White Star liner *Queen Mary*.

In the engine room, now known as the machinery space, the bases for boilers and for machinery would be fitted by the shipyard, and then the engineering department would commence the erection of engines and the complementary and vital task of boring out the aperture for the propeller shaft. Here accuracy was paramount, and this work had to be done without extremes of temperature that might cause shaft misalignment. Lastly the masts, cranes, derricks and deck gear had to be fitted, rigged and tested for safe operation.

A woman assistant to a riveting team during the Second World War.

A revolutionary change took place in the twentieth century when a new method of joining steel was introduced; known as welding, this system enabled plates to be joined without an overlap, and rivets to be discarded, giving a 10 per cent saving in structural weight. In the 1920s and 1930s, the novelty of their skill enabled

A riveting team in Aberdeen in the 1940s.

Shipyard machine tools: plate rollers to the left and guillotine and plate cutter to the right.

Probably the first all-welded hull ever built – the barge *Ac1320*, constructed by the Royal Engineers at Richborough in Kent and launched in June 1918.

welders to claim wages above the norm; they regarded themselves as the leaders of the shop floor.

The idea of bonding metal using electric current had been around for a long time, and the system was mastered in Sweden in 1906 using a welding rod of

Welding opened the way for complex prefabricated structures in shipbuilding. This shows a completed bulbous bow ready for incorporation in the hull structure.

The mould loft at Vickers Shipyard at Barrow-in-Furness around 1910. Here the ship is drawn out full size on the floor and all working templates produced.

Near-complete unit assemblies await transport and then erection.

A well-completed unit of a new ship under construction in Belfast.

sacrificial material that melted in an electric arc between the two plates to be bonded together. It is probable that the first ship to be 100 per cent welded was a barge built and launched by the Royal Engineers at the military port of Richborough, Kent, in 1918, while the world's first sea-going all-welded hull was the motor vessel *Fullagar*, built at Birkenhead by Cammell Laird in 1920. Welding had a slow introduction into British shipbuilding as during the inter-war years the market price for ships was so low that capital investment was indefinitely postponed. Further, with large numbers of unemployed riveters clamouring for work, there was little incentive to change from riveting to welding.

Painting was another area of change. Gone are the days when fabrications were wire-brushed and coated with red lead or other primers and then covered with conventional paints. Painting in the open air, exposed to wind, rain and frost, is redundant, and steel units are now shot-blasted in specially constructed and enclosed shops before being moved to paint spray booths where temperature and humidity are controlled as special paint systems, which may last four or more years, are applied. (Current research on paint and similar protective coatings is aimed at achieving a guarantee of ten years without recoating – a remarkable objective as this will enable ship hulls to be repainted perhaps only twice in their full working lives – with massive savings in cost.) This has enabled the shipyards to construct pre-assembled units of from 50 to 800 tonnes with all parts fitted and with painting complete apart from the small strip where pre-assembled units are joined to each other by welding.

This change came about when (in the 1950s) it was appreciated that costs escalated in a shipyard if work was moved several times during construction. A slightly exaggerated rule of thumb was that the cost of work in the assembly shops was tripled if carried out on the building berth, and then tripled again if carried out afloat. With this principle established, most modern shipyards try to have no more than three moves in the construction pattern: first, preparing the items for assembly; second, constructing the units and ensuring every part is incorporated and paintwork complete; finally, the units have to be lifted by overhead crane to an outfitting dock for final assembly before the flooding of the dock and the floating out of the ship. History was made in the 1960s when one large ferry was built in five units that were 'stitched' together before floating and almost immediate delivery.

A view of the main mast of the four-masted barque *Pommern*, now preserved at Mariehamn in the Åland Islands in the Baltic Sea. Not only is the rigging impressive, but the steel masts and spars are well structured.

The SS *St Sunniva* on trials off Aberdeen in 1931. This beautiful ship was lost in 1943 while acting as a convoy rescue ship.

SHIP LAUNCHING

ONE OF THE MOST dramatic ship launches ever took place at Clydebank, near Glasgow, in 1934. The sponsor was the wife of King George V, and this new liner, one of the largest ships in the world, was privileged to have her name – *Queen Mary*. When the formalities were complete and a bottle of champagne had been broken against her hull, the great liner was released and 38,000 tonnes of ship and shipyard equipment moved backwards into the River Clyde, gaining speed until checked by the drag chains, and then stopped safely afloat at a point exactly 365 metres from her place of build. The whole operation took a mere 100 seconds, and for a short time the hull was travelling backwards at a speed of more than 20 miles per hour. The naval architect of John Brown's shipyard received great acclaim, especially when it came to light that, through meticulous research and design work, his team had estimated the ship's travel accurately to within 0.5 metre.

Traditionally, British-built ships are launched stern first and slide down two 'ways' on a cement apron or hard-packed inclined ground with a 'declivity' or slope of around 1 in 17. During construction of the ship, two broad timbers (known as 'standing ways') are laid beneath the hull and anchored to the ground. When the standing ways are secure they are greased, and 'sliding ways' are run under the ship and positioned, and a cradle is built between them and the hull. The ship and its supporting cradle will slide into the water on the standing ways. A few days before the launch, work starts on transferring the weight of the ship from the supports on which it was built to the cradle and the launchways. The final task, a few hours before the launch, is to 'ram up' the ship: finely tapered wedges are hammered home to ensure the ship is fully supported by the cradle and ready to move. To prevent the ship sliding ahead of schedule, the sliding ways are held secure by triggers or daggers which on release allow the ship to move backwards into the water. This system has been in use since the eighteenth century, and the first known drawings of such arrangements were made in 1768 by the Swedish naval architect Fredrik Henrik af Chapman, the son of a British officer in the Royal Swedish Navy. When all

Opposite:
The launch party for the SS *Changsha* at Scott's of Greenock, 1883. The scale of the vessel is clear when compared with the profile drawing on the next page.

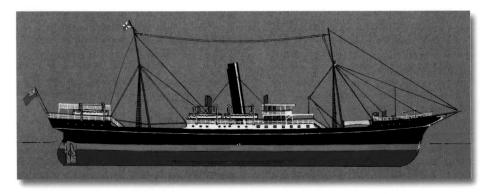

The SS *Changsha* of 1883.

The launch party for HM Offshore Patrol Vessel *Shetland* at Aberdeen in 1976.

is ready, it is usual to find that the hull has moved a few millimetres down the slipway, and this is described as the ship 'being alive'.

In the hours before launch all equipment on the ship is secured carefully, lifesaving appliances are placed aboard, the men aboard are listed and their tasks detailed. This precaution dates back to 1883, when a coaster, the SS *Daphne*, overturned in the Clyde immediately after launch. In the official enquiry a few weeks later, it was established that nearly two hundred persons

had been aboard, all at work to ensure completion of the ship within a few days. It transpired that the stability had not been checked, and on touching the water the ship heeled over, a list from which the ship might have survived had it not been that 30 tons of men and loose equipment slid over the decks resulting in the capsize of the vessel and the loss of 124 lives.

The task of sponsoring a new ship is regarded as an honour, and usually the future owners (in consultation with the builders) invite a lady to perform the naming. The flags on the ship reflect the nationality of the builders as the ship belongs to them until completed, and hence one can see the apparently anomalous situation wherein a new ship, say for Norway, with 'Bergen' painted on its stern, enters the water flying the British Red Ensign, but always with the Norwegian flag on the 'courtesy position' of the foremast.

The Royal Navy has different launching ceremonies, and the ship is dressed with just three flags: the Union Flag ('Union Jack') forward, the White Ensign at the stern, and the Lord High Admiral's flag on the highest mast. The wine must be from a Commonwealth country, not champagne from Britain's former great rival at sea, France. The sponsor has to be approved by the Queen and it is the hope of all shipyards that she herself will grace their yard at some time, or at least will send one of her close family. It is believed that the first religious service at a launching was requested by Alexandra, Princess of Wales, for the ironclad battleship *Alexandra* at Chatham Dockyard in April 1875. Nowadays such services are regular features of all naval launches and have become frequent for merchant ships.

The most dramatic launches are into narrow rivers or canals. Here the ship is built alongside the water's edge and then launched sideways, a system that was used in parts of Britain until the late twentieth century, but is now seen in only a few countries, including the United States, Germany and the Netherlands. Instead of two long launchways, the site has seven or eight short ones, and

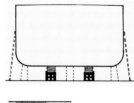

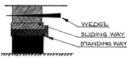

WEDGE
SLIDING WAY
STANDING WAY

Top: A cross-section of a ship under construction. The permanent or 'standing' ways are shown in solid black, while the shaded timbers are the sliding ways on which the ship is cradled.

Left: Details of the ways, showing the wedge that, when pressed home, transferred the weight of the ship to the launchways. In modern times more sophisticated methods are used, but the basic principle remains unaltered.

Below: Details of the traditional wooden dagger that has been used for the last three hundred years in launchways throughout the world.

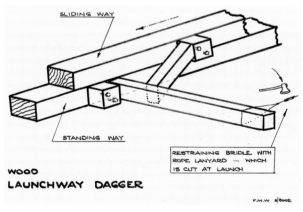

SLIDING WAY

STANDING WAY

WOOD
LAUNCHWAY DAGGER

RESTRAINING BRIDLE WITH ROPE LANYARD — WHICH IS CUT AT LAUNCH

F.M.W. 2/2002

The trawler *Aberdeen Distributor* hits the water in 1958.

Sideways launches were once common in Britain, especially where shipyards were on the side of a narrow waterway or canal. This picture shows the United States Army Logistic Ship *MG Robert Smalls* being launched in Mississippi in 2004.

it is vital that the many daggers are released simultaneously or it is possible that the ship will slide in a skewed manner, become stuck on the ways, or, worse, capsize on entry to the water.

The days of 'dynamic' or sliding launches are almost over; nowadays many ships are built in docks, and the launching is little more than the flooding of the dock. Others, including the great submarines now built at Barrow-in-Furness, are rolled out of the construction hall and on to a ship-lift, which gently lowers them into the sea — still dramatic to watch but lacking the excitement of older times.

WORKING CONDITIONS

B Y TODAY'S STANDARDS, life was fairly tough for workers in a shipyard of the nineteenth or early twentieth century. While conditions varied slightly from yard to yard and from district to district, everyone working 'outside' in the main part of the shipyard was employed on an hourly basis, with little sense of security and with little in the way of a pension to look forward to. Older men, often afflicted by deafness – a common occupational hazard, dreaded the time when they would have to stop work and live on whatever small savings they had accrued.

In 1916, on the River Tyne, a man's working hours amounted to fifty-four in the week. Six days a week, work started at 6 a.m. and continued until 5 p.m., except on Saturdays, when they finished at 12.10 p.m. There was a break for breakfast from 8.30 to 9 a.m., and another for lunch from 12.30 till 1.20 p.m. Each man was allowed a total of eight days paid holiday, including Christmas, Easter and New Year's Day. Much of the work was out of doors, with little cover. Canteens, mess rooms and washing places were non-existent, and lavatory facilities were of the most primitive nature, often little more than a walled shelter enclosing a plank with suitably sized holes cut a metre apart and draining to the nearest river or dock.

In the works regulations for Palmers of Jarrow there is an ominous entry with regard to inquests following a fatal accident: 'The Manager of the Department affected is the direct representative of the Company in the case, and must attend the Enquiry in question. He must take care that he is accompanied by the Company's Solicitor.' This underlines the fatalistic approach to death in the shipyards, an emotional feeling that continued almost until the early 1950s – that every large ship inevitably was the cause of the death of one workman.

Starting in the late nineteenth century, most yards organised sickness and injury funds, often financed partly by grants from the shipyard owners and partly by small weekly contributions (possibly a few pennies) from each employee. From this small start, interest grew (albeit slowly) in health, welfare and above all safety. Backing was given by ever-improving health and

Overleaf: A view from the bridge of the Cunard liner *Queen Elizabeth* while afloat and fitting out, probably in early 1939. Work has only started on the decks and deck fittings. The town of Clydebank, to the west of Glasgow, was developed from a green field site in the nineteenth century, and until recently had only two main employers: the John Brown shipyard and the Singer Sewing Machine Company, whose tower can be seen in the distance.

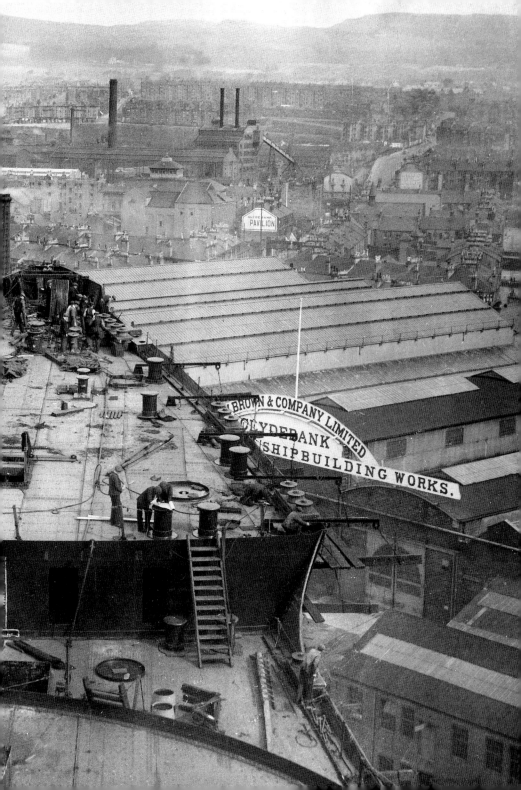

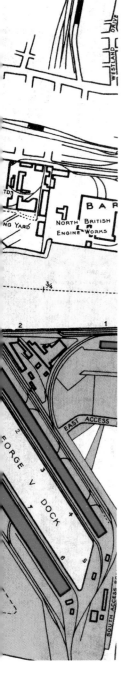

safety legislation, and in the 1960s by the Shipbuilding Regulations. Every shipbuilding site in Britain now has proper first-aid areas and employs at least one full-time manager with the task of a dedicated approach to safety and risk assessment.

Insecurity of employment was one of the most vexed subjects in the long and complex history of British shipbuilding. The need to protect the interests of each trade led to the imposition of demarcation on the work floor whereby each group of workers defined their tasks in great detail. Blame cannot be placed solely with the workers as employers from time immemorial were happy to contract specific or defined jobs to groups of tradesmen for an agreed price. This system, known as piecework, eased the short-term requirements of management, but did little to address the real problem. Shipbuilding suffered from no more or no fewer disputes than any other heavy industry in Britain, or indeed in Europe, until the mid-twentieth century, but the word demarcation acquired negative overtones. Since the 1960s much progress has been made in developing interchangeability between trades to even out the workflow, and there has been a virtual merging of the workforce and a vast reduction in the number of trade unions involved.

One part of this history was almost forgotten – the Fairfield Experiment, which commenced after the financial collapse of the Fairfield shipyard at Govan in 1965. This brought about a new semi-nationalised company with investment from government, industry and some also from the trades unions. Over a two-year period there were some fascinating changes, although sadly the experiment was never completed owing to the merger of the Upper Clyde shipyards, which overtook events. Whether or not one agreed with all that happened, it did change the way shipbuilders communicated, bringing a merging of trades and a significant reduction in the numbers of trades unions.

A plan of some of the shipyards in the upper reaches of the River Clyde around 1960. All these yards (but one – Yarrows) have closed, a situation in some part owing to the restrictions on space caused by nearby housing and the enclosing effect of both roads and railway track. It can be seen that building berths are inclined to the river to enable the construction of the largest possible size of ship hull.

TESTING AND
TRIALS

The heavy-lift ship
Duburg having her
Hallen derrick
tested prior to
delivery in 1967.

ONE OF THE MOST exciting parts of any shipbuilding programme is the testing and trials of the new ship. As modern ships are of great complexity, the task of gathering all the certification and documents is a massive procedure in its own right, and many shipyards employ special departments, or sometimes subcontractors, to see this job through. While the ship is on the building berth, every part is tested for watertight integrity, and the whole structure is examined in close detail by the shipyard's own quality assessors and by the surveyors of Lloyd's Register or one of its rivals. When the ship is afloat, it is subjected to an 'inclining experiment' to ensure it is safe and stable while afloat. It is allowed to float free in calm waters, and a series of weights is moved in a prearranged manner while the ship's angle of heel is recorded; this is analysed in the naval architect's office, and the ship's stability particulars are issued to the owners. These stability characteristics must meet the most stringent international statutory requirements. The ship is dry-docked and a last coating of protective paint (known as 'anti-fouling') is applied to the underwater hull. Today this coat of paint may be guaranteed for many years.

Finally the ship moves out to commissioning trials, during which every item of the equipment and machinery is tested rigorously, and the ship's ability to manoeuvre and to come to an emergency stop is recorded. Two other vital tests have to be made: first, the efficiency of the anchors, and the ability of the ship's windlass to recover the anchors and chain cables from the bed of the sea; and second, the obligatory adjusting of the compass. Every ship develops a magnetic field while being built on the ground, and the compass has to be adjusted as close as possible to magnetic north; any small discrepancies have to be recorded and posted in the wheelhouse for the navigating officers to see.

The days are over when new ships were leaving the great rivers of Britain perhaps not quite every day, but certainly several times a month. While this is sad, one thing is sure – the quality of ships built in Britain has never been higher. The shipbuilders of Britain build their vessels with justifiable pride.

The bulk carrier *Erradale*, built by Harland and Wolff of Belfast, on trials in 1994.

The Royal Fleet
Auxiliary tanker
Wave Ruler
awaits launching
at Govan in 2001.

CLASSIFICATION SOCIETIES AND QUALITY ASSURANCE

The phrase '100A1', indicating that something is excellent, above reproach and of the highest quality, has a maritime background. It is recorded against the entry of a ship's name in the international list known as Lloyd's Register. This great organisation, which has been associated with ships and shipbuilding for more than 250 years, originated in 1760 as an informal group of people with shipping interests who all frequented Edward Lloyd's coffee shop in London. From this has grown an organisation with more than eight thousand employees and offices in over eighty countries, and which has the task of ensuring that ships (and other industrial structures) comply with Lloyd's stringent rules and also international legislation. Lloyd's appoints surveyors to almost all shipyards, and also to steelworks, to ensure ships built under their inspection qualify for their endorsement. The famous Register of Ships published by Lloyd's and others is a compendium of almost every ship in the world – the 2007–8 edition had four volumes, comprising 7,600 pages of entries with the technical details of more than 95,000 ships.

FURTHER READING

Abell, Sir Westcott. *The Shipwright's Trade*. Cambridge, 1948. A masterly overview of ship design and construction through the ages.

Af Chapman, Fredrik Henrik. *Architectura Navalis Mercatoria*. Stockholm, 1768. There have been many facsimile editions of this superb book, which displays the draughtsmanship skills of a pioneer naval architect.

Arnold, A. J. *Iron Shipbuilding on the Thames 1832–1915: An Economic and Business History*. Aldershot, 2000.

Fincham, John. *A History of Naval Architecture*. London, 1851; also facsimile edition, 1979.

Landström, Björn. *The Ship*. Stockholm, 1961.

MacDougall, Philip. *Royal Dockyards*. Newton Abbot, 1982.

Walker, Fred M. *Song of the Clyde: A History of Clyde Shipbuilding*. Cambridge, 1984.

Walker, Fred M. *Ships and Shipbuilders: Pioneers of Ship Design and Construction*. Barnsley, 2010.

Winchester, Clarence (editor). *Shipping Wonders of the World*. London, c. 1938. The bound two-volume edition of a popular maritime magazine of the 1930s.

Two historical novels, both by George Blake, can also be recommended: *The Constant Star*, and *The Shipbuilders*. They describe the life of shipbuilders, first in the confident pioneering nineteenth century, and then in the economic depression of the 1930s.

The chemical tanker *Orionman* on trials. Note the complexity of the pipework on deck. Paintwork has yet to be completed.

PLACES TO VISIT

Aberdeen Maritime Museum, Shiprow, Aberdeen AB11 5BY.
   Telephone: 01224 337700. Website: www.aagm.co.uk
Chatham Historic Dockyard, Chatham, Kent ME4 4TE.
   Telephone: 01634 823807. Website: www.thedockyard.co.uk
   (HMS *Gannet*, HMS *Cavalier* and HM Submarine *Ocelot*.)
Cutty Sark Clipper Ship, King William Walk, Greenwich, London SE10 9HT.
   Website: www.rmg.co.uk
Denny Ship Model Experiment Tank, Castle Street, Dumbarton G82 1QS.
   Telephone: 01389 763444.
   Website: www.museumsgalleriesscotland.org.uk/member/denny-ship-
   model-experiment-tank
Discovery Museum, Blandford Square, Newcastle upon Tyne, NE1 4JA.
   Telephone: 0191 232 6789.
   Website: www.twmuseums.org.uk/discovery
Gloucester Waterways Museum, Llathony Warehouse, The Docks, Gloucester
   GL1 2EH. Telephone: 01452 318200.
   Website: www.gloucesterwaterwaysmuseum.org.uk
SS Great Britain at the Great Western Dockyard, Gas Ferry Road, Bristol, BS1 6TY.
   Telephone: 0117 926 0680. Website: www.ssgreatbritain.org
Hartlepool Maritime Museum and HMS *Trincomalee*, Maritime Avenue,
   Hartlepool, TS24 0XZ. Telephone. 01429 860077.
   Website: www.hartlepoolsmaritimeexperience.com
HMS Belfast, Queen's Walk, London SE1 2JH.
   Website: www.iwm.org.uk/visits/hms-belfast
HM Frigate Unicorn, Victoria Dock, Dundee DD1 3JA.
   Telephone: 01382 200 900. Website: www.frigateunicorn.org
Hull Maritime Museum, Hull City Council, Queen Victoria Square, Hull
   HU1 3DX. Telephone: 01482 300 300. Website: www.hullcc.gov.uk
Merseyside Maritime Museum, Albert Dock, Liverpool Waterfront, Liverpool
   L3 4AQ. Telephone: 0151 478 4499.
   Website: www.liverpoolmuseums.org.uk/maritime
National Maritime Museum, Park Row, London, Greater London SE10 9NF.
   Telephone: 020 8858 4422. Website: www.rmg.co.uk
National Maritime Museum Cornwall, Discovery Quay, Falmouth, Cornwall
   TR11 3QY. Telephone: 01326 313 388. Website: www.nmmc.co.uk
National Maritime Museum of Ireland, Old Mariners Church, Haigh Terrace,
   Dun Laoghaire. Telephone: 01 280 0969.
   Website: www.dun-laoghaire.com
National Museum of the Royal Navy, Portsmouth. (HMS *Victory*, the warship
   Mary Rose and HMS *Warrior*.)

Pannet Park Museum, Pannet Park, Whitby, North Yorkshire, YO21 1RE.
Telephone: 01947 600933. Website: www.pannettpark.co.uk

Riverside Museum, 100 Pointhouse Place, Glasgow, G3 8RS.
Telephone: 0141 287 2720.
Website: www.glasgowlife.org.uk/museums/our-museums/riverside-museum (and the three-masted barque *Glenlee*.)

Scottish Maritime Museum, 6 Gottries Road, Irvine, Ayrshire KA12 8QE.
Telephone: 01294 278283. Website: www.scottishmaritimemuseum.org

Submarine Museum, Haslar Jetty Road, Gosport, PO12 2AS.
Telephone: 023 9251 0354. Website: www.submarine-museum.co.uk (Many pioneer boats.)

The Titanic Experience, Titanic Quarter, Queen's Island, Belfast, N. Ireland BT3 9DT. Telephone: 028 9076 6386. Website: www.titanicbelfast.com

Wool House Maritime Museum, Town Quay, Southampton, Hampshire SO14 2AR. Telephone: 023 8063 5904. Website: www.southampton.gov.uk /s-leisure/artsheritage/museums-galleries.

The motor side trawler *Spinningdale* leaves Aberdeen on its first voyage; it was built by John Lewis of Aberdeen in 1968.

INDEX